Pizza: Theme and Variations

PIZZA

THEME AND VARIATIONS

By Rita Blinderman

DRAWINGS BY
Becky Anderson

THE STEPHEN GREENE PRESS

BRATTLEBORO, VERMONT

To the memory of

my mother, a great cook

This book has been produced in the United States of America.

IT IS PUBLISHED BY THE STEPHEN GREENE PRESS, BRATTLEBORO, VERMONT 05301.

LIBRARY OF CONGRESS CATALOGING IN PUBLICATION DATA

Blinderman, Rita, 1940-
  Pizza: theme and variations

    Includes index.
    1. Pizza. 2. Cookery, International. I. Title.
TX770.B54 1980   641.8′24   79-19115
ISBN 0-8289-0357-3

Contents

1

INTRODUCTION

$\mathbb{P}$IZZA is another word for pie. Its basis is a circular bread-like disc, bordered by a rim that encloses combinations of tomato sauce, cheese and meat. The pizza has become an American institution, joining franks and hamburgers among our naturalized national dishes. Pizzerias have sprung up throughout the land. Baking companies have created scores of pizza mixes. Frozen food companies have profited handsomely by putting pizza on ice. Teenagers have made the local pizzeria a social gathering place. Rushed mothers bless the pizza when they have to improvise a meal on short notice. The pizza is indeed a part of our national life. It has enlarged our economy, modified our social patterns and encouraged amateur and professional chefs to add exciting dishes to our cuisine.

The conquest of America by the pizza began with the conquest of Italy by the Allies in the Second World War. American G.I.'s stationed in southern Italy developed a taste for the traditional Neapolitan pizza, which was eaten as a light repast during social get-togethers in local pizzerias. The pizza passion mushroomed in the United States on the return of our servicemen after the war.

Although the pizza is the Italian–American dish *par excellence*, other countries have their distinctive versions of the same treat. The Armenian *Lahmejoun* or *Missahatz*, the French *Pissa-ladière*, even the popular

Jewish *Matzoh*, are, in their own ways, variations on the pizza idea. Many national variations on the pizza are described in this book, for the enjoyment of all pizza aficionados.

You can invent your own pizza specialties by varying doughs and fillings. Mix and match some of the fillings and sauces in this book, and combine them with the basic doughs described. The many doughs, the different fillings, the varied sauces, should inspire you to embark upon your own Pizza Experience.

Buon appetito!

HELPFUL INFORMATION

The wonderful aroma of pizza at the pizzeria is exciting to the palate. Few people take the time to try to make pizza at home, however, perhaps because they think it's harder than it really is. In fact, making pizza takes less time than making bread: pizza has fewer ingredients, its creation requires fewer steps. Anyone who loves pizza can make pizza.

Before attempting to make pizza, read the information below. You'll understand better how to proceed, and you'll have a better product.

Flour. The flour used in all the recipes is all-purpose flour unless stated otherwise. It should be sifted before measuring. When making dough, try to keep it as soft as you can handle. Add only enough additional flour, when necessary, to keep the dough from sticking to your hands. This is done before the rising period.

Yeast. You may substitute compressed yeast for dry yeast if you wish, but it should be dissolved in warm water (85 degrees F.). Packaged dry yeast is dissolved in water at a higher temperature (105–115 degrees F.). A candy or room thermometer is helpful in dissolving the yeast.

Sugar. Most of these recipes contain some sugar. It contributes to the manufacture of gas bubbles by the yeast and enhances the flavor of the pizza dough.

Salt. Salt is helpful in controlling the yeast's action. It also adds flavor.

Shortening. Shortening allows the dough to expand easily. Fat adds flavor and tenderness to the dough and assists in the browning process. Butter, margarine, vegetable shortening, salad oil or lard may also be used in the basic dough recipes. Solid fats must be melted before using.

Kneading. To knead, place the dough on a floured surface, such as a large cutting board. Slap it down. Take the edge furthest from you and bring it toward the edge nearest you. Relax your hands over the dough and push away firmly with the heels of your hands. Use a light touch and rolling motion. Turn the dough around slightly and repeat this procedure over and over. Always turn the dough in the same direction. Knead at least five minutes, or until the dough is smooth and elastic.

Rising. Place the dough in a lightly greased bowl and turn it over. This will grease the top. Cover the dough loosely with a light cover, such as a cloth, to prevent the top from crusting. Place bowl in a draft-free location with about an 85-degree temperature (F.). An ideal spot is an unlit gas oven. Put a large bowl of hot water on the oven floor, and place the dough in its bowl on the oven shelf above. Close the oven door and let the dough rise for 60 minutes or until it has doubled in bulk. Punch the risen dough down by pushing your fist into the center of the dough and folding the dough into the middle of the bowl. If you wish you may let the dough rise again for another half hour. Punch down again after the second rising. The dough is now ready for shaping. (The second rising is not strictly necessary, but it does improve the dough.)

Shaping. Flatten the dough out with your hands. If you're handy at flinging it around and stretching it to size in midair with the tops of your fists as the experts do in the pizzerias, fine. However, a rolling pin or your finger tips will do a good job too. Roll the dough out to fit the size of your pan, about a quarter of an inch thick. Place the dough on a pizza pan or cookie sheet, leaving a lip at the edge to hold the filling. Some pizzerias sprinkle a little corn meal, alone or mixed with flour, on the greased pan before baking.

Baking. Before baking the pizza, line the bottom of the oven with aluminum foil to catch any possible drips. Place the oven shelf in the lowest possible position in the oven. Pre-heat the oven to the temperature given in the chosen recipe. When the proper temperature is reached, place the greased pie pan in the center of the rack and bake until the dough is a golden brown and the sauce bubbly. When the recipe calls for a partially or fully pre-baked shell, pour enough dried beans or rice into the uncooked pie to prevent the dough from rising in the center during pre-baking. For a partially pre-baked shell, bake for 5–7 minutes. To fully bake the shell only, bake for 12–15 minutes, or until golden brown.

Equipment. For small pies use a regular 8- or 9-inch pie pan, round, or a layer cake pan. For larger pies the 12-inch pizza pans or the disposable pans are useful. If you come across the 16-inch pan your recipe will have to be increased proportionally. Cookie sheets are handy for the square pies, thick or thin. You will need two bowls—one for mixing ingredients in and one in which to allow the dough to rise; a measuring cup for the flour and water; measuring spoons; a mixing spoon; covering cloth; and a flat area such as a large cutting board to work on. To cut the finished pizza, a cutting wheel is recommended, but a sharp knife will do.

Pizza Bricks. The authentic way to cook pizza is on a stone. It disperses the heat evenly and imparts a superior flavor to the dough. The crust is crispy on top and bottom, while the dough inside remains moist.

You can reproduce this method of baking pizza in your electric or gas oven by purchasing unglazed quarry tiles. They usually are about 5½ inches square. The Yellow Pages of your telephone book will have a listing of quarries, tile companies or lumber yards to choose from.

Nine tiles fitted on the lowest shelf of the oven serve the purpose. If the oven measures to 16½ inches square or more, the tiles will fit. Otherwise, 6 tiles will fit most ovens for smaller size pizzas.

Prepare the pizza for baking. Sprinkle a tablespoon of corn meal over the hot tiles (500 degrees F.). Place the pizza directly on the hot tiles.

Pizza Paddle. In handling pizzas in the oven, the paddle serves to keep the shape of the pie intact, and to protect the face and hands from heat. The paddle may be purchased in most department stores. I bought mine in Macy's. It's about 19 inches long and 13 inches across at its widest point, with a handle at one end. After the pie is baked, remove from the oven with the paddle onto a pie plate.

Pizza has become so popular to the homemaker that the department stores are now carrying a **pizza kit**. The kit consists of a 13-inch round, lightweight pizza brick, pizza handle, pizza rack and pizza cutter. The name of the manufacturing company is Bricks Unlimited, Inc., 3140 N. 25th Street, Terre Haute, Indiana, 47804.

2
BASIC DOUGHS

PREPARATION of pizza dough is a simple operation. Basic dough is the result of combining flour, yeast, water, sugar and salt in proper proportions. To create variations of the basic dough is merely a matter of adding other ingredients to the five components mentioned.

The thickness of the dough is a matter of individual taste. For a thick, bread-like base, use a cake pan or a pie plate as a substitute for the regular pizza pie pan. For square pizzas try using the smaller square cake pans. If you prefer a thinner dough, use a regular pizza pan or a cookie sheet. Since cooking is an art, you might enjoy experimenting with utensils that suggest other pleasing forms for your pizzas.

The basic pizza doughs described in this chapter may be used with any of the fillings that are listed in the chapter on fillings. You may decide on the conventional pizza topping, or you may explore other possibilities suggested in the International section. There are countless variations. With imagination, you can create mouth-watering ideas of your own.

Basic Dough I

MAKES TWO 12-INCH PIES

1 package active dry yeast
1 cup warm water (105–115 degrees F.)
3 cups flour (about)
1 teaspoon sugar
½ teaspoon salt
2 tablespoons olive oil
1 tablespoon corn meal (optional)

Soften yeast in warm water. Mix in 1½ cups flour; add sugar, salt, oil, and the rest of the flour. Knead until smooth and elastic. Grease bowl, place dough inside, then grease dough surface and cover with cloth. Let rise in a warm place, about 85 degrees F., until double in bulk—about 1½ hours. Punch down, roll out on floured surface to fit two 13-inch round pie pans (sprinkle pans with corn meal before baking). Push the sides of the dough up about half an inch to hold filling. The dough is now ready to be filled and baked at 450 degrees for 15–20 minutes, or until the crust is a golden brown.

Basic Dough II

MAKES THREE 12-INCH PIES

2 packages active dry yeast
½ cup warm water (105–115 degrees F.)
1½ cups milk (105–115 degrees F.)
¼ cup olive oil
1 tablespoon sugar
1 teaspoon salt
5 cups all-purpose flour (about)

Sprinkle yeast into warm water and dissolve. Mix warm milk, oil, sugar and salt with yeast. Beat in 4 cups flour; add more gradually for a soft dough. Knead until smooth and elastic. Grease large bowl, place dough inside, turn dough around to grease top. Cover with cloth and let rise in a warm place, about 80–90 degrees, until doubled—about 45 minutes to an hour. Punch in the middle with your fist. Turn onto a flat surface and divide dough into three balls. Stretch each into 12-inch pie pans, leaving a half-inch lip at the edge to prevent filling from spilling out. (For a thicker dough use smaller pans.) Fill with desired filling and bake on the lowest oven shelf at 450 degrees for about 45 minutes or until crust turns golden brown.

VARIATION: SICILIAN PIZZA CRUST

A favorite in Southern Italy, the Sicilian dough is actually a thick-crusted bread-like dough. Prepare the regular Basic Dough I recipe for two pies. Instead of making two pizzas, make one large one. Pat or roll out the dough to fit on a greased cookie sheet or jelly roll pan. Grease the top and let dough rise in the pan about 20 minutes more, in addition to the regular rising period. Keep covered in a warm place during that time. Prepare filling. Fill and bake at 425 degrees for about 15 or 20 minutes, or until crust turns golden brown. Cut into squares and serve hot.

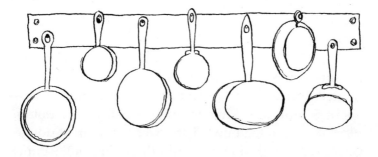

Royal Dough

1 package active dry yeast
1 cup warm water (105–115 degrees F.)
1 egg (beaten)
¼ cup olive oil
4 tablespoons mashed potato
3 cups flour
2 teaspoons sugar
1 teaspoon salt

Dissolve yeast in warm water. After the yeast is dissolved add the egg, oil and mashed potato. Combine dry ingredients and mix into liquid. Place dough on floured surface and knead until smooth and elastic— about 5 minutes. After forming a ball of the dough, place it in an oiled bowl. Turn over to oil top of dough. Cover with cloth. Let rise until double in bulk. Punch down after 1½ hours. Cut in half for two 13-inch pies. Roll out on floured board and press into well-oiled pie pans. Push side up half an inch to hold filling. Dough is now ready to be filled and baked in 450-degree oven until golden brown—about 15–20 minutes.

VARIATION:

Sprinkle chopped nuts, grated Parmesan cheese, sesame or other tasty seeds, dried onion or garlic flakes, singly or in your own combination onto a greased baking sheet. Press dough on top of ingredients and continue with filling and baking, as above.

Makes a rich, flavorful, homestyle dough.

Whole Wheat Pizza Dough

MAKES TWO 12-INCH PIES

1 package active dry yeast
1 cup warm water (105–115 degrees F.)
2 cups (approximately) all-purpose flour
1 cup whole wheat flour
2 tablespoons molasses
1½ teaspoons salt
5 tablespoons olive oil or salad oil

Follow the directions for Basic Dough I.

VARIATIONS:

Instead of whole wheat flour substitute other flours such as rye, graham, corn meal, buckwheat, or soy.

Honey, maple syrup, corn syrup or sugar may replace the molasses.

Corn oil, safflower oil, or other table oils may be used instead of olive oil.

For a quick dough use whole wheat bread mix. The mix saves about 10–15 minutes from beginning to end.

A nutritious dough, full of vitamins.

Herb Pizza Dough

MAKES ONE 12-INCH PIE

2 tablespoons olive oil
or other oil
½ cup warm water
(105–115 degrees F.)
1 package active dry
yeast
1¼ cups sifted
all-purpose flour
1 teaspoon sugar

½ teaspoon salt
1 tablespoon onion
flakes
1 teaspoon sage
½ teaspoon thyme
½ teaspoon caraway
seeds or poppy
seeds

Combine oil and water. Add yeast to warm liquid and let stand 5 minutes. Sift flour, salt and sugar together. Add herbs to flour mixture and combine all ingredients. Mix well, then place dough on a floured surface and knead until smooth and elastic. Form a ball and place in an oiled bowl; turn over to oil top. Cover with cloth and let rise in a warm place—about 85 degrees F.—until double in bulk. After rising, punch

18

dough down in center; place on floured board. Sprinkle a well-oiled 12-inch pizza pan or 10-by-15-inch rectangular sheet with corn meal. Roll out dough and fit into chosen utensil. Build a half-inch lip at edge of pizza to keep filling in. Pizza is now ready for desired topping. Bake on bottom shelf of oven at 450 degrees for 15–20 minutes or until crust turns golden brown and filling is bubbly.

VARIATION:

Replace the herbs suggested above with others of your own choosing. Replace onion flakes with garlic flakes. Use crumpled rosemary instead of sage. Add 1 tablespoon chopped parsley instead of one of the herbs, or in addition to the herbs. Sesame seeds or other seeds may replace recipe seeds. A little grated cheese and a few chopped nuts add to the taste.

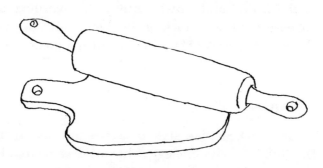

Hot Roll Mix Crust

MAKES ONE 12-INCH PIE

Use this time-saving preparation, found in the super-market, as you would any of the Basic Dough recipes above. All necessary ingredients are included in the package.

Grease a 12-inch pizza pan or a 15-by-10-inch cookie sheet or jelly roll pan. Pat the prepared dough onto the pan. Make a small lip at edge of pan to hold filling. For an interesting design, clip edges at one-inch intervals, or dent edges with knuckles at even intervals. Fill with desired filling. For fast results, use a can of pizza sauce as the filling and finish with your favorite topping. Bake on the lowest rack of the oven at 425 degrees for about 20 minutes or until edges turn a golden brown.

VARIATIONS:

For a thick Sicilian-style pizza use the basic recipe for Hot Roll Mix with one egg. This makes a regular bread-like dough. Let it rise once. If you find the dough a bit too sticky when patting it into the baking pan, sprinkle with a little flour for easier handling. Bake on lowest shelf of oven at 400 degrees until crust is golden brown.

To vary the pizza dough or the bread dough, add any of the following to the flour preparation before mixing with the liquid: ½ cup grated Parmesan cheese; ¼ cup chopped nuts or seeds; 2 tablespoons dried onion flakes or garlic flakes; 1 tablespoon dried herbs such as oregano, basil or parsley.

Standard Pastry Dough

2 cups sifted all-purpose flour
1 teaspoon salt
¾ cup vegetable shortening
4 to 6 tablespoons water (start with 4 and add as
    needed)

Combine flour and salt in bowl. Cut in shortening
until mixture resembles small peas. Two knives, a pastry blender or a low-speed electric mixer will cut the
shortening into the flour. Slowly sprinkle water into the
mixture while mixing with fork, until ingredients are
evenly moistened. At this point, shape dough into a
ball, wrap in wax paper and refrigerate until ready to
roll out; or gather mixture together with hands and
press firmly into a ball, roll out, and shape as indicated
in individual recipe. This pastry is rolled ⅛ inch thick.
Place in pie pan, prick dough with fork, and top with
favorite filling. Bake in a preheated oven (425 degrees)
until crust turns golden brown.

VARIATIONS:

Divide dough into five sections. Roll each part into a 4-inch circle for small pizzas, pizza tarts or pizza muffin cups. Prick surface with fork before baking.

Roll dough to ⅛-inch thickness. With a drinking glass cut out circles for pizza canapes. Prick surface with fork before baking.

Use fancy-shaped cookie cutters for fancy party mini-pizzas.

Cut 3-inch circles from rolled pizza dough. Turn custard cups or muffins pans upside down, grease lightly, lay circles on top of each cup. Pleat circle to fit each cup shape evenly, prick with fork. Bake and fill with prepared filling; or wrap, freeze and store for future use.

Cheese Pastry.   Use Standard Pastry Dough as base. Change amount of flour from 2 cups to 1⅔ cups of sifted flour. Add ¾ cup grated sharp Cheddar cheese or grated Parmesan cheese. Continue with recipe as directed.

Nut Pastry.   To Standard Pastry Dough recipe add ½ cup chopped nuts.

Any of the items below may also be added to the above dough. Mix one or more with dry ingredients:

1 tablespoon dried herbs in combination or separately—oregano, basil, etc.

1 tablespoon garlic flakes, less if you prefer

1 tablespoon onion flakes
3 tablespoons chopped salami
1 tablespoon seeds, such as sesame, sunflower, caraway, poppy or your choice
¼ cup crushed, canned, fried onion rings plus an additional tablespoon water
¼ cup chopped popped corn plus an additional tablespoon water
1 teaspoon freshly ground black pepper

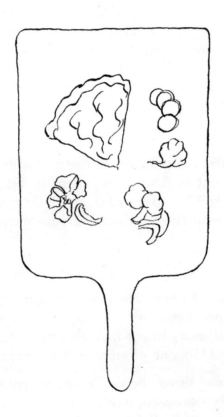

PIZZA: THEME AND VARIATIONS

Rice Pizza Crust

1 cup boiled rice
1 cup milk
1 egg, beaten
½ cup Parmesan cheese, grated
1 cup flour
¼ cup cornstarch
1 heaping teaspoon baking powder
½ teaspoon salt

Mix rice with milk and well-beaten egg. Add Parmesan cheese and stir. Sift dry ingredients and mix gradually into milk mixture. Stir in enough more milk to make thin batter (about 4 tablespoons). Bake on hot, greased griddle until golden brown on both sides. Top with your favorite filling and sauce.

This recipe gives you a delicious use for leftover rice.

Pasta Pizza

½ pound pasta: broad noodles, spaghetti or
  elbow macaroni
1½ cups scalded milk
1 cup soft crumbs
¼ cup Parmesan cheese, grated
¼ cup butter or margarine
1 tablespoon chopped onion
3 eggs, beaten
1 teaspoon salt

Cook noodles according to package directions. Drain.
Add all other ingredients. Pour into large pie pan
which has been thoroughly greased. Place pie on center
shelf of oven with a pan of hot water underneath.
Bake at 350 degrees for 50 minutes or until crust is
browned. Serve with pizza sauce and any of the following: mushrooms, anchovies, tuna, fried onions and
peppers, pepperoni, or fried Italian sausage. Sprinkle
with Parmesan cheese and serve. Serves six.

Polenta Pizza

1 cup corn meal
1 cup cold water
1 teaspoon salt
4 cups boiling water

Combine corn meal, cold water, and salt. Stir. Place boiling water in top part of a double boiler. Stir corn meal mixture in gradually. Cook and stir over high heat for 2–3 minutes. Cover and steam over, not in, hot water about 15 minutes, stirring frequently. Turn polenta into greased 12-inch pie plate. Top with tomato sauce and chosen topping—try sausage, cheese, mushrooms, or onions. Bake in preheated 450-degree oven for 15–20 minutes, or until heated through.

Semolina Pizza

1 quart milk
3 tablespoons butter
1 cup semolina or farina
⅔ cup Parmesan cheese, grated
2 eggs, beaten
1 teaspoon salt

Heat milk and butter on low flame until butter melts. Add semolina, stirring constantly. (If mixture gets too thick, stir in a little more milk.) Remove from heat and blend in cheese. Pour eggs into mixture, stirring constantly. When smooth in texture, spread into greased pizza pan, elevating edge half an inch to hold filling. Fill and bake in a 450-degree oven until thoroughly heated through (15–20 minutes).

Quick Biscuit Dough

MAKES ONE 12-INCH PIE

2 cups flour
1 tablespoon baking powder
1 teaspoon salt
⅓ cup oil
¾ cup milk

Sift dry ingredients; mix in milk and oil. Stir until a ball is formed. Knead on a lightly floured board about a dozen times. Roll out dough between 2 sheets of waxed paper. Place in 12-inch pie pan, or try a square pan such as a cookie sheet. Spread with desired topping. Bake at 425 degrees for about 15 minutes until dough is lightly browned.

VARIATIONS:

Add one of the following to dry ingredients before mixing in liquids:

½ cup crumbled bacon

⅓ cup bleu cheese, crumbled; or shredded gouda cheese

⅓ cup grated sharp Cheddar cheese and 1 tablespoon instant onion flakes

⅓ cup grated sharp Cheddar cheese and 1 teaspoon garlic flakes

⅓ cup grated Parmesan cheese and 1 tablespoon chopped parsley

⅓ cup (either) caraway, poppy or sesame seeds

⅓ cup (either) chopped walnuts, pecans or almonds

1 teaspoon oregano, basil, dill or chives, chopped

Quick Little Pizza

1 package refrigerator biscuits
1 can tomato sauce with onions
¼ pound Muenster cheese, sliced
grated Parmesan cheese
oregano

Pre-heat oven to temperature indicated on package. Flatten biscuits with palm of hand and place on cookie sheet. Top each biscuit with tomato sauce, a piece of Muenster cheese, a sprinkling of Parmesan cheese, and a pinch of oregano. Bake until biscuits turn golden brown and cheese begins to bubble.

Individual Pizza
à la English
Muffins

1 package English muffins
1 slice of Muenster cheese for each muffin
1 tablespoon tomato sauce for each muffin
1 slice anchovy or pepperoni for each muffin
oregano
Parmesan cheese

Split muffins. Rub each side with garlic on the hard surface (optional). Spread tomato sauce on each, a slice of cheese, an anchovy or pepperoni slice, a sprinkling of oregano, Parmesan cheese, and a little olive oil. Bake in 400-degree oven until cheese melts, about 10–15 minutes.

Fritter Pizzas

MAKES 4 TO 6 SERVINGS

2 eggs, beaten
1 cup milk
½ cup Parmesan
  cheese
1 tablespoon melted
  shortening
2 cups sifted flour

3 teaspoons baking
  powder
½ teaspoon salt
1 cup chopped onion,
  chopped tomato or
  eggplant
½ cup oil for frying

Combine beaten eggs, milk, Parmesan cheese and shortening. Sift dry ingredients and gradually combine liquid ingredients. Stir until batter is smooth; add vegetables. Heat oil in skillet. Drop batter by tablespoonfuls into hot oil. When fritters are browned on both sides, remove and drain on absorbent paper. Serve with tomato sauce and additional Parmesan cheese.

Pita Pizza

1 package dry yeast
½ teaspoon sugar
1 cup warm water (100–115 degrees F.)
⅛ cup oil
2 level teaspoons salt
3 cups bread flour, approximately
2 tablespoons corn meal

Add yeast and sugar to ½ cup warm water in a large mixing bowl. Let stand 5 minutes while measuring flour, oil and salt. Stir in the other ½ cup of warm water, add the oil, salt and 2½ cups of flour. Turn out the dough (which may be sticky) on a floured board and gradually knead in the remaining flour. If the dough is still too sticky to handle, add a little more flour. Don't overdo the flour. Knead 5 minutes or more, until the dough becomes elastic and smooth. Place ball of dough in an oiled bowl. Turn around to coat with oil.

Cover with tin foil or cloth and let rise in a draft free, warm place until double in bulk, about 1½ hours.

Place fist onto center of dough to punch down. Shape into ball again and divide into 5 equal parts. Transfer balls to an oiled cookie sheet and cover with cloth. Let rise again for ½ hour, then roll out each one to about 5 inches. Sprinkle 2 oiled cookie sheets with one tablespoon corn meal each. Place 3 pitas on each sheet. Let rise again for another 25 minutes.

Place one cookie sheet on lower shelf of very hot oven (500 degrees F.) for 5 minutes, at which time no peeking, until the time is up. Now open the door and place pan on higher shelf, from 3 to 5 minutes. When the pitas blow up like balloons and are very light brown, remove from oven. Place the second cookie sheet in the oven using the same procedure as the first. The pitas will deflate when cool. Wrap the loaves in plastic or foil until ready to use to insure soft pita texture. These breads split open to form a pocket. Fill them with any of the fillings in the book, hot or cold.

Pita is a Middle Eastern bread which splits easily into two layers.

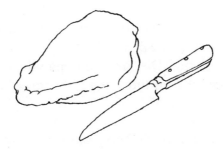

Low Calorie Jiffy Dough

1 cup powdered skim milk
1 egg
¼ teaspoon salt
pepper to taste
1 teaspoon water
1 teaspoon oil
2 tablespoons flour

Combine all ingredients and mix well but leave excess flour out in a small flat dish. Form a ball of combined ingredients. If the ball is sticky, use the flour to help press the dough out into the oiled pie plate by putting your fingers into the flour and pushing the dough into place. Spread the dough as far as it will go without tearing. Discard the remainder of the flour.

Prebake for 8 minutes in a 350-degree F. oven before filling.

If you are allergic to flour products, or just wish to avoid too many calories, try this.

3
SAUCES

PIZZAS have a tongue-tingling array of sauces that add to the pie's attractiveness as well as to its savory substance.

Even if you don't have time to create in the kitchen, you can choose from a fine selection of prepared sauces at the supermarket or deli. A slight pause for heating, and—*presto*—you are ready to saucify your pie.

Tomato Sauce I

3 tablespoons coarsely chopped onion
1 minced garlic clove
1 eight-ounce can tomato purée
2 tablespoons olive oil
1 teaspoon of oregano
salt and pepper to taste

Sauté onion and garlic in heated oil for 2 minutes. Add the rest of the ingredients and cook 15 minutes over moderate heat.

Tomato Sauce II

3 cups plum tomatoes, peeled and chopped (may
  be fresh or canned)
1 teaspoon salt
1 teaspoon oregano
¼ teaspoon pepper
2 tablespoons olive oil

Mix all ingredients together and bring to a boil. Serve.

This is a simple, quick sauce.

Tomato Sauce III

¼ cup olive oil
1 medium onion,
   chopped
1 clove garlic, minced
1 carrot, chopped
2 stalks celery,
   chopped
1 green pepper,
   chopped
3 cups tomato purée

1 tablespoon tomato
   paste
¼ cup fresh basil,
   chopped; or 2
   teaspoons dried
   basil
5 sprigs fresh parsley,
   chopped; or 2
   tablespoons dried
   parsley

Sauté onion and garlic in oil until golden. Add carrot, celery, and green pepper and cook for 10 minutes, stirring occasionally. Add tomato purée, tomato paste, and seasonings. Simmer over low heat for 40 minutes.

Try this versatile sauce over pasta or on pizza.

Tomato Sauce with Meat and Sausage

MAKES ENOUGH FOR TWO 13-INCH PIES

3 tablespoons butter
3 tablespoons olive oil
2 slices bacon, chopped
2 medium onions
1 chopped garlic clove
½ lb. chopped meat
½ pound sausage meat, removed from casing and chopped
2 cups canned plum tomatoes or fresh plum tomatoes, chopped

¼ cup chopped mushrooms
½ cup water
8 parsley sprig leaves, chopped
½ teaspoon basil
½ teaspoon peppercorns
1 tablespoon tomato paste
½ cup dry white wine
1 tablespoon Parmesan cheese, grated

Heat butter, oil, and bacon in large skillet; add onions and garlic and fry gently until golden. Add chopped meat and sausage to skillet; brown 10 minutes more. Add the water, tomatoes, mushrooms, and seasonings, reserving the tomato paste, wine, and cheese. Cook over medium-low heat for 1½ hours, stirring occasionally. Add tomato paste, wine, and Parmesan cheese. This sauce is also delicious over pasta.

Uncooked Tomato Sauce

MAKES ENOUGH FOR TWO 13-INCH PIES.

3 cups drained, squeezed tomatoes
½ teaspoon salt
sprinkling of pepper
1 teaspoon oregano
¼ teaspoon basil
2 tablespoons olive oil

Mix all ingredients together. Spread on top of pizza dough and add preferred topping (cheese, anchovies, mushrooms, onions, etc.) in addition to the tomatoes. Bake for about 30 minutes at 450 degrees on a 13-inch pie pan or on a cookie sheet.

VARIATION:

To the Uncooked Tomato Sauce recipe above add the following:

2 tablespoons fresh chopped basil
¼ cup chopped parsley
1 clove garlic, minced
½ cup dried, sautéed bacon

Mix all ingredients with Uncooked Tomato Sauce. Simmer over medium heat for about 15 minutes. Use over any dough. Makes enough for two 13-inch pies.

Eggplant Pizza Sauce

MAKES ENOUGH FOR TWO 13-INCH PIES

1 medium eggplant, peeled and cubed
1 large onion, cut up
1 cup sliced mushrooms
½ teaspoon garlic salt
1 teaspoon oregano or basil
salt and pepper to taste
2 cups tomato purée
¼ cup olive oil

Sauté eggplant, onion, and mushrooms in olive oil over medium heat. Add the rest of the ingredients when onions look transparent. Simmer 30 minutes. Use over any pizza dough, with or without cheese.

Tomato Sauce with Chopped Beef and Chicken

MAKES ENOUGH FOR THREE 12-INCH PIES

½ cup olive oil
¼ cup bacon, cut into little pieces
4 medium onions, chopped
2 garlic cloves, minced
¾ lb. chopped beef
½ lb. chicken pieces
1 large can plum tomatoes or fresh plum tomatoes, chopped

1 cup hot water
1 crushed bay leaf
½ teaspoon rosemary
1 teaspoon peppercorns
2 teaspoons fresh chopped parsley
1 teaspoon salt
¼ cup Burgundy wine

Heat oil and bacon in skillet; add onions and garlic and sauté gently until golden. Add the beef and chicken and cook for 5 minutes; add the remaining ingredients except the wine. Cook for 1 hour, stirring occasionally. Add the wine during the last 10 minutes of cooking.

In addition to pizza topping this sauce can be used over your favorite pasta dish.

Tomato-Tuna Sauce
(with Ricotta or
Green Beans)

MAKES ENOUGH FOR TWO 13-INCH PIES

¼ cup butter
¼ cup olive oil
4 medium onions,
  chopped
2 garlic cloves, minced
2 cups tomatoes

3 tablespoons tomato
  paste
¼ teaspoon pepper
4 chopped anchovies
1 seven-ounce can
  tuna

Choice of one:
2 cups green beans—fresh, or frozen defrosted
½ cup ricotta cheese or creamed cottage cheese

Heat butter and oil in large skillet; add onions and garlic and sauté over medium heat until golden brown. Add tomatoes, tomato paste, and seasoning. Simmer over low heat for 30 minutes. Mix in tuna, anchovies, and green beans or ricotta. Cook for 5 minutes more.

Marinara Sauce

MAKES ENOUGH FOR TWO 13-INCH PIES

¼ cup butter
¼ cup olive oil
½ cup chopped parsley leaves
2 garlic cloves, minced
1 cup canned or fresh plum tomatoes, chopped
2 tablespoons tomato paste
6 anchovy fillets, mashed
1 teaspoon oregano

Heat butter and oil in skillet. Add parsley and garlic. When the garlic turns golden brown, add the remaining ingredients. Simmer for 30 minutes.

Marinara Sauce with Onions

MAKES ENOUGH FOR THREE 12-INCH PIES

¼ cup butter
¼ cup olive oil
2 cups chopped
 onions
1 small carrot chopped
3 garlic cloves, minced
1 bay leaf

4 cups plum tomatoes,
 fresh or canned
½ teaspoon oregano
½ teaspoon basil
2 tablespoons tomato
 paste
salt and pepper to taste

Heat butter and oil in skillet; add onions and sauté until golden. Add carrot and chopped garlic; sauté 5 minutes. Add the remaining ingredients; cook for 30 minutes. Put the sauce through a sieve or purée in blender and return sauce to skillet to cook for another 30 minutes, on a medium-low flame.

Vinaigrette Sauce

1 cup olive oil
2 hard-boiled eggs,
coarsely chopped
1 garlic clove, minced
juice of one lemon
6 tablespoons wine
vinegar
3 coarsely mashed
anchovies (optional)

1 teaspoon capers
1 chopped scallion
1 teaspoon fresh dill
½ teaspoon freshly
ground black
pepper
salt to taste

Combine all ingredients; beat well. If the sauce is not for immediate use, leave the garlic out until the last minute. Refrigerate the dressing and add the garlic when ready to serve.

VARIATION:

Eliminate the eggs and replace with 4 tablespoons crumbled Roquefort cheese.

White Clam Sauce

MAKES ENOUGH FOR ONE 13-INCH PIE

2 dozen cherrystone
 clams
1 medium onion,
 chopped
3 tablespoons butter
2 cloves garlic,
 chopped
¼ cup parsley,
 chopped

1 tablespoon
 all-purpose flour
¼ teaspoon dried
 thyme or basil
salt and pepper to taste
¼ cup dry white wine

Clams should be thoroughly scrubbed before open-ing. Open the clams by cutting the muscle or putting them in the oven at a high heat until they open by themselves. This procedure only takes a few minutes. As soon as the clams open, remove from the oven. Remove the clams from the shells and chop. Set the liquid aside.

Sauté onion in butter until golden, then add garlic and parsley; cook another 3 minutes. Blend in flour and stir well. Add clam liquid and seasonings. Add wine. Bring to a boil and remove from heat immediately.

Red Clam Sauce

MAKES ENOUGH FOR TWO 13-INCH PIES

2 cups tomato sauce
1 cup chopped clams,
   fresh or canned
2 minced garlic cloves
¼ cup chopped
   parsley
1 teaspoon thyme or
   basil

1 tablespoon tomato
   paste
1 tablespoon
   all-purpose flour
salt and pepper to taste
½ cup olive oil

See instructions on how to open clams in White Clam Sauce recipe on preceding page. Chop the fresh clams and reserve liquid; if canned clams are used, no preparation is necessary. Heat oil and lightly sauté garlic and parsley without browning. Blend flour into mixture, stirring while adding tomatoes, canned clams, and seasonings. If the fresh clams are used, add them, with the clam juice, at the last minute. Bring to a boil and remove from flame.

4

TRADITIONAL
FILLINGS
AND TOPPINGS

I N the classic pizzeria, pizza is prepared in the presence of the hungry customers. The most popular toppings are mushrooms, onions, sausages and green peppers, singly or in combination. The selected topping is strewn over a layer of tomato sauce or chopped, peeled and seeded tomatoes sprinkled with herbs. The fragrant pizza is baked until the crust acquires a delicate brown hue; then the pizza is removed from the oven. It is best to cut the hot pie into wedges immediately. Hold the slice of pizza in a napkin while consuming the pie from its tender tip to its crunchy base.

SUGGESTED TOPPINGS FOR PIZZA

Choose as many in combination or as few as desired. Most of the suggestions are used with pizza sauce as a base, but this isn't always necessary.

Cheese. Cheddar, Parmesan, Muenster, cottage cheese, mozzarella, bel paese, feta cheese, swiss cheese, ricotta, romano. Or try your own favorites.

Fish. Anchovies, sardines, tuna fish, cooked or canned shrimp, caviar, lox, sturgeon, whitefish, smoked eel, herring fillet (pickled matzes or schmaltz), fresh fillet pieces, clams, oysters, lobster, kippers. Any canned or smoked fish.

Meat. Prosciutto; chicken livers, plain or chopped; Italian sausage, sweet or hot, cooked; linked sausage, cooked; brown-and-serve sausage or loose sausage meat, cooked; meatballs, canned or cooked; hamburger; frankfurters, canned or grilled; pieces of cooked chicken or turkey; cold cut strips, including salami, cooked ham, corned beef; pastrami, bologna, liverwurst; smoked tongue.

Nuts. Slivered toasted almonds; chopped peanuts; chopped walnuts; pine nuts; toasted pumpkin seeds; sesame seeds; sunflower seeds; chopped cashew nuts; chestnuts.

Vegetables. Asparagus tips, canned or cooked; escarole; broccoli; zucchini stir fried in oil for 2 minutes; raw or fried onions; mushrooms, canned, fried or pickled; pimientos; green pepper, fried or raw; pickled artichokes; cucumber pickles and pickled vegetables; ripe Greek or Italian pitted olives; fresh or canned sliced tomatoes; chick peas; any canned or cooked bean; chopped garlic; sauerkraut; herbs, including oregano, basil, parsley, chives, dill, thyme, etc.

Cheese Topping

1 large can Italian
plum tomatoes,
drained, chopped
and squeezed
1 teaspoon sugar
granulated garlic to
taste, or fresh chopped
garlic (optional)
salt and pepper to
taste

2 twelve-inch unbaked
pizza shells
1 eight-ounce package
mozzarella cheese,
shredded
basil
oregano
⅓ cup Parmesan
cheese
2 tablespoons olive oil

Mix tomatoes with sugar and seasoning. Spread on dough shells. Sprinkle mozzarella cheese on top and basil and oregano to taste. Cover with Parmesan cheese. Drizzle oil over all and bake in preheated oven at 450 degrees on the lowest shelf for 15 to 20 minutes or until crust and bottom turn golden brown. Serve at once.

VARIATION: ANCHOVY TOPPING

Use 16 anchovy strips, and anchovy oil in can instead of olive oil in the Cheese Topping recipe. Place anchovy strips on cheese in pinwheel fashion.

Add remaining ingredients and bake as directed.

VARIATION: ONION TOPPING

6 large sweet onions, Spanish type, sliced thinly
½ cup olive oil

Using Cheese Topping recipe, sauté onions in hot oil gently, until transparent but not brown. Spread on top of cheese. Add remaining ingredients and bake as directed.

VARIATION: GREEN PEPPER TOPPING

3 medium green peppers, sliced into ¼" rings
½ cup olive oil

Use Cheese Topping recipe. Sauté peppers in hot oil for 5 minutes over medium heat. Arrange on top of two pies, over the mozzarella cheese, then add remaining ingredients and bake as directed.

VARIATION: MUSHROOM TOPPING

Use 2 cups partially sautéed fresh mushrooms, or more if you wish. Using Cheese Topping recipe above, sprinkle mushrooms on top of mozzarella. Add remaining ingredients and bake as directed.

VARIATION: SAUSAGE TOPPING

Using the Cheese Topping recipe, sprinkle 1 pound sausage meat, removed from its casing and crumbled, over the mozzarella. Add remaining ingredients and bake slightly longer than directed for the Basic Recipe.

VARIATION: PEPPERONI TOPPING

Use 8 ounces of pepperoni, thinly sliced. In the Cheese Topping recipe, arrange pepperoni slices on top of mozzarella. Add remaining ingredients and bake.

VARIATION: MEATBALL PIZZA

Use one 8-ounce can meatballs, or 12 homemade meatballs. Adapting Cheese Topping recipe, slice meatballs or cut them in half, and scatter over mozzarella cheese. Add remaining ingredients and bake as directed.

VARIATION: SALAMI TOPPING

8 ounces Italian salami or other salami, cut into
   ½" chunks
¼ pound prosciutto or ham, cut into little pieces
½ cup sliced mushrooms (1 three-ounce can,
   drained)

In the Cheese Topping recipe, sprinkle mozzarella
with salami and prosciutto or ham. Add remaining
ingredients and bake as directed.

VARIATION: CHOPPED MEAT PIZZA

1½ pounds chopped meat or leftover meatloaf
2 tablespoons olive oil
1 clove garlic, minced
½ cup sliced mushrooms (1 three-ounce can,
   drained)

In the Cheese Topping recipe, sauté beef in oil until
half done. Drain fat. Mix in garlic and mushrooms.
Sprinkle on top of mozzarella cheese and add remaining ingredients. Bake as directed. If using meatloaf,
crumble it over the cheese, mix the canned mushrooms
with the garlic and scatter them over the meat. Bake as
above.

Clam Filling

MAKES ONE 12-INCH PIE

1 ten-ounce can
  minced clams
1 cup plum tomatoes,
  drained and
  chopped
2 tablespoons
  chopped parsley
  leaves

½ teaspoon thyme
1 chopped garlic clove
¼ cup chopped onion
salt and pepper to taste
1 uncooked pie shell,
  12 inches
1 cup mozzarella
  cheese, shredded

Drain clams, save liquid for soup, combine all ingredients except mozzarella cheese. Spread over pie shell. Sprinkle cheese over top, Bake in 450-degree oven on bottom shelf, about 20 minutes or until crust is lightly browned.

VARIATIONS:

Replace the clams with 1 cup small shrimp, lobster chunks, crabmeat pieces or coarsely-chopped oysters.

Low Calorie Filling

¾ cup chopped tomatoes, fresh or canned, drained
½ teaspoon onion powder
½ teaspoon oregano
salt and pepper to taste
½ cup any skim milk cheese, farmer, baker or hoop cheese
1 tablespoon Parmesan cheese (optional)
3 or 4 fresh basil leaves (optional)

Mix first four ingredients and spread over top of pie. Sprinkle cheeses on top, arrange basil leaves on pie and place in oven for 8 to 10 minutes, until hot.

VARIATIONS:

Add any vegetables you prefer, sliced mushrooms, onions, peppers, etc. Other fillings in the book are tasty with this pie crust. The choice is yours.

5
PIZZA
ELABORATIONS

AS you continue your pizza exploration, discovering the pleasures of making your own pies, you will also discover one of the pizza's chief virtues—versatility. The pizza is a theme that lends itself to endless variations. The balance of this book will indicate the range of possibilities for pizza transformation.

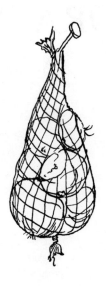

　　　　　　　　　　　PIZZA: THEME AND VARIATIONS

Tuna Pizza

MAKES ONE 13-INCH PIE

2 seven-ounce cans
   chunk style tuna,
   drained
¼ cup chopped
   onion or
   scallion
2 tablespoons
   chopped green or
   red pepper
¼ cup chopped
   parsley or celery (or
   both)

1½ tablespoons
   lemon juice or
   wine vinegar
1 cup shredded
   mozzarella cheese or
   crumbled feta cheese
½ cup mayonnaise
2 medium tomatoes,
   sliced
1 twelve-inch pie shell,
   unbaked

Mix all ingredients together, except the tomatoes. Fill pie shell. Arrange tomato slices over top along edge of pie. Bake on the lowest shelf of 450-degree oven for 15 to 20 minutes, or until crust turns golden brown and cheese melts.

VARIATIONS:

Use canned salmon instead of tuna.

Sprinkle ¼ cup grated Parmesan cheese over top of pie before baking.

Pour one cup tomato sauce over surface of pie before baking.

Sprinkle 1 can of sliced mushrooms or sautéed fresh mushrooms over top of pie before baking.

Sprinkle 1 teaspoon oregano or basil on top of pie before baking.

Tuna Chili Pizza

MAKES ONE 12-INCH PIE

1 package hot roll mix
1 tablespoon butter or
   margarine
¼ cup chopped onion
1 clove garlic, minced
¼ cup chopped green
   pepper
¼ cup chopped celery
1 tablespoon chili
   powder
1½ teaspoons sugar
½ tablespoon salt
¼ teaspoon dried leaf
   oregano

¼ teaspoon dried leaf
   basil
1 bay leaf
1 eight-ounce can
   tomato sauce
1 one-pound can
   tomatoes, drained
2 cans (6½ or 7 ounces
   each) tuna in
   vegetable oil
1 cup shredded
   Monterey Jack
   cheese

Prepare hot roll mix according to package directions
for pizza crust. Pat into a 12-inch pizza pan. Let rise

while preparing sauce. Melt butter in large saucepan. Add onion, garlic, green pepper and celery. Cook until tender, about 5 minutes. Add chili powder, sugar, salt, oregano, basil, bay leaf, tomato sauce and drained tomatoes. Simmer, uncovered, for 30 minutes. Add tuna. Spread over pizza dough; sprinkle with cheese. Bake in a 425-degree oven for 30–40 minutes or until crust is golden brown.

Chicken Liver Pizza

MAKES ONE 12-INCH PIE

3 tablespoons olive oil
1 large chopped onion
1 pound chicken livers
1 cup tomato sauce
½ teaspoon oregano
½ teaspoon basil

¼ teaspoon garlic salt
1 chopped hard-boiled egg
1 unbaked pizza pie shell (12 inches)

Sauté onion in oil until transparent. Add chicken livers and continue to cook until browned. Chop livers coarsely. Add tomato sauce and seasonings to liver and onion mixture. Oil pie shell (1 tablespoon oil), and spread liver and tomato over surface. Bake in 450-degree oven until dough turns golden brown. Sprinkle chopped egg over surface and serve.

A special treat for liver lovers.

Summer Pizza

1 twelve-inch pie shell, freshly baked
3 large tomatoes, sliced
1 Bermuda onion, sliced, or 3 scallions, sliced into
  small pieces
2 tablespoons fresh basil or 1 tablespoon dried
¼ teaspoon garlic salt
¼ cup olive oil
2 tablespoons wine vinegar
¼ teaspoon salt

Fill pie shell with sliced tomatoes, placed evenly. Scatter onion rings or scallion pieces over tomatoes. Sprinkle basil and garlic salt over top. Mix olive oil, vinegar and salt together and sprinkle over all. The pie is now ready to eat.

VARIATIONS:

Instead of oil and vinegar dressing, try the Pizza Sauce on the next page or the Vinaigrette Sauce on Page 52.

Sprinkle the top with ¼ cup Parmesan cheese.

Scatter bits of anchovy pieces on top.

Try crumbled Roquefort cheese or feta cheese sprinkled over surface.

Add cut-up meats such as pepperoni slices, ham bits, sliced salami or any other desired cold cuts.

Small shrimp, pieces of tuna, sardines or herring may also be scattered over the tomatoes.

Summer Sauce

MAKES ONE 12-INCH PIE

½ cup tomato sauce
¾ cup olive, corn, or safflower oil
3 tablespoons wine vinegar
½ teaspoon oregano
½ teaspoon basil
4 tablespoons Parmesan cheese
1 garlic clove, minced
salt and pepper to taste

Combine all ingredients in jar. Shake well and set aside for a while until flavors mingle. Mix again before using.

VARIATIONS:

Add one can anchovies, cut into small pieces, with their oil.

Instead of Parmesan cheese, use crumbled feta cheese.

Add 2 tablespoons chopped onion.

Add 2 tablespoons of chopped parsley or 1 tablespoon of chopped dill to dressing.

Add 2 tablespoons pignoli nuts to sauce.

Ricotta Cheese Pie

1 recipe for Basic Dough I (2 crusts)
3 pounds ricotta cheese
3 eggs
½ pound mozzarella cheese, diced
3 tablespoons Parmesan cheese
1 pound Italian sausage meat, removed from casing and cooked
¼ pound ham or prosciutto
salt and pepper to taste

Mix ricotta, eggs, mozzarella, and Parmesan. Add meats and season to taste. Stretch or roll dough into 2 circles to fit a 12-inch shallow casserole dish. Line the greased dish with 1 circle of dough. Pour ricotta mixture into shell and cover top with other circle. Press edges together and trim off excess dough. Flute edge; make slits on top for steam to escape. Bake at 400 degrees for 15 minutes, then lower temperature to 325 degrees for 35 to 45 minutes. Allow pie to cool a few minutes before cutting.

Escarole Pizza

MAKES ENOUGH FOR 4–6 SERVINGS

1 recipe Basic Dough I
(2 crusts)

3 small escaroles,
parboiled and
shredded

¼ cup olive oil

1 crushed garlic clove

2 tablespoons capers

6 anchovy fillets,
sliced into pieces

6 coarsely chopped
black olives

2 tablespoons pine
nuts

salt and pepper

Cook escarole in oil with garlic, salt, and pepper for 10 minutes. Divide dough into 2 parts. Stretch 1 part to cover bottom of greased, 12-inch shallow casserole dish. Spread escarole over dough. Sprinkle with capers, anchovies, olives, and pine nuts. Stretch other piece of dough over top. Press edges together; trim off excess dough. Flute edge; make slits on top to allow steam to escape. Bake at 375 degrees for 35 to 45 minutes.

Casatiella

MAKES 6–8 SLICES

1 dough recipe
4 eggs, hard-boiled, shelled and halved
2 tablespoons butter or oil
salt and pepper to taste
2 tablespoons chopped onion or 2 teaspoons garlic
  granules

Shape dough into large bagel or doughnut form. Press 8 egg-shaped holes on top, at even intervals. Set half an egg in each opening. Pinch dough together over eggs and brush with butter or oil. Sprinkle with seasoning, including a sprinkling of onion or garlic on top, if desired. Bake on greased 9-inch pizza pan in 350-degree oven from 35 to 45 minutes until golden brown.

Cheese and Onions

½ lb. Cheddar cheese or mozzarella, shredded
1 large Bermuda onion, thinly sliced and fried in
   oil 5 minutes
6 slices half-cooked bacon
2 tablespoons mayonnaise
1 teaspoon prepared mustard
½ teaspoon oregano
salt and pepper to taste
1 pizza dough recipe

Combine all ingredients except bacon. Spread over dough. Arrange bacon slices in pinwheel fashion on top. Bake in 450-degree oven for about 20 minutes or until cheese melts and crust is golden brown.

Caponata Pizza

2 cups canned caponata
½ cup Italian peppers cooked in oil
1 pizza dough recipe
6 ½-inch-thick slices broccoli cut lengthwise
¼ cup olive oil
¼ cup Parmesan cheese
2 tablespoons pine nuts
salt and pepper to taste

Mix caponata with peppers, spread on dough. Cook broccoli lightly in oil for 10 minutes, in skillet. Arrange lengths on pie in pinwheel fashion. Sprinkle with Parmesan cheese and pine nuts. Season to taste. Bake in preheated 450-degree oven for about 20 minutes or until crust turns golden brown.

Avocado Filling

2 ripe avocados
3 tablespoons
  mayonnaise
3 tablespoons tomato
  paste
1 tablespoon lemon
  juice or vinegar
touch of tabasco sauce
2 tablespoons
  chopped onion

2 cloves chopped
  garlic
tomato slices (enough
  to decorate pie)
1 12-inch prebaked
  pizza pie shell, just
  baked
salt and pepper to taste

Mash avocados. Blend in mayonnaise, tomato paste, lemon juice or vinegar, tabasco, onion and garlic. Spread over pie surface. Decorate pie with tomatoes. Serve immediately.

Zucchini Pizza

MAKES ONE 12-INCH PIE

1 garlic clove, minced
3 tablespoons olive oil
1 cup tomato sauce
3 tablespoons tomato
   paste
1 teaspoon salt
½ teaspoon pepper

2 tablespoons fresh
   basil
3 medium zucchini,
   sliced
1 twelve-inch pie
   shell, prebaked

To serve cold, add garlic to hot olive oil, and cook for 3 minutes. Add rest of ingredients. Bring to a boil and cook in covered skillet for 15 minutes. Cool and spread on pie surface.

VARIATION:

Garnish pie with ¼ cup ripe black olives and 6 strips of anchovies.

VARIATION:

To serve hot, sprinkle ½ cup mozzarella cheese over top and ¼ cup Parmesan cheese over all. Place pie in 450-degree oven for a few minutes until the cheeses melt.

If desired, add a few anchovies in pinwheel fashion on top of cheeses before placing in oven.

Yogurt-Onion Pizza

MAKES ONE 13-INCH PIE

8 sliced onions
¼ cup butter or
   margarine
2 lightly beaten eggs
1½ cups plain yogurt
½ teaspoon oregano

¼ teaspoon garlic salt
salt and pepper to taste
½ cup grated cheese
1 unbaked 13-inch pie
   shell

Sauté onions in butter or margarine over low heat until transparent. Mix eggs, yogurt and seasonings together. Spread onions over pie shell; pour yogurt mixture over onions. Sprinkle grated cheese over top. Bake for 20 minutes or until crust turns golden brown (450-degree oven).

Pizza Ratatouille

MAKES ONE 12-INCH PIE

1 onion, chopped
1 garlic clove, minced
¼ cup olive oil
1 small eggplant,
    diced
1 medium zucchini,
    diced
½ green pepper, diced
1 small can tomato
    sauce

1 teaspoon oregano
1 teaspoon basil
salt and pepper to taste
¼ cup Parmesan
    cheese
1 twelve-inch pie
    shell, unbaked

Sauté onion and garlic in olive oil until transparent.
Mix in eggplant, zucchini, and green pepper and sauté
for 10 minutes. Blend in tomato sauce and seasonings.
Cover and simmer for 30 minutes. Remove cover and
cook 20 minutes more. Spread mixture over pie shell.
Sprinkle Parmesan cheese over top. Bake in 450-degree

oven for 20 minutes, or until pie shell turns golden brown.

An interesting combination of herb-seasoned vegetables on pizza dough.

VARIATION:

Sprinkle 1 cup mozzarella cheese over ratatouille and bake as directed.

Crab Thermidor Pizza

MAKES TWO 12-INCH PIES

2 cups crabmeat,
  cooked and cleaned
½ cup sliced
  mushrooms
4 chopped scallions
2 peeled, chopped,
  tomatoes
2 tablespoons butter

2 tablespoons sherry
1 cup sweet cream
3 egg yolks, beaten
salt and pepper to taste
2 twelve-inch pie
  shells, freshly baked

Combine crabmeat, mushrooms, scallions, and tomatoes; cook in butter 10 minutes. Beat cream into yolks. Mix a few tablespoons of the hot ingredients into the egg mixture, then stir all together in skillet. Add sherry. Cook over low heat until thickened, stirring constantly. Pour into prebaked shell. Serve hot. Sprinkle a tablespoon of parsley on top for color.

Lobster Newburg Filling

MAKES ONE 12-INCH PIE

2 cups cubed lobster
  meat
2 tablespoons butter
½ cup sherry
2 tablespoons brandy
½ cup cream
3 egg yolks, slightly
  beaten

dash of cayenne and
  nutmeg
salt and pepper to taste
1 twelve-inch pie shell,
  freshly baked

Cook lobster in butter for 3 minutes; add sherry and brandy, cook another minute. Beat cream into yolks, then mix a little of the hot mixture into it. Combine all ingredients in skillet, add seasonings, and cook until mixture thickens, mixing constantly. Don't overcook or sauce will curdle. When thickened, remove from heat immediately. Pour onto prepared pie shell. Sprinkle with paprika and serve. Choose any variety of dough as a base.

Meat Leftovers

MAKES ONE 12-INCH PIE

2 cups leftover meat,
   fish or poultry, cut
   into pieces
1 medium onion,
   chopped
½ cup sliced
   mushrooms
1 cup chopped plum
   tomatoes

2 tablespoons
   chopped parsley
1 chopped garlic clove
salt and pepper to taste
¼ cup olive oil
1 twelve-inch pie shell

Mix all ingredients. Cook in hot oil for 10 minutes in heavy skillet. Bake on a 12-inch pie shell of regular pizza dough, hot roll mix dough or biscuit dough in 450-degree oven for 15 or 20 minutes, or until dough is golden brown.

This recipe is flexible. Substitute any meat, fish or poultry to produce a number of thrifty dishes.

Pizza Toast

1 cup shredded mozzarella or other cheese
¾ cup drained canned plum tomatoes, chopped
½ cup chopped onion
dash garlic salt and oregano
8 slices white bread

Mix cheese, tomatoes, onion and seasonings and re-frigerate. When ready to serve, pre-heat oven to 450 degrees. Toast and butter bread. Spread tomato mixture on top. Bake 10 to 12 minutes until cheese melts. Cut into triangles and serve.

Pizza Sandwiches

4 long Italian rolls
1 small can pizza sauce
12 small meat balls (canned or homemade)
4 slices muenster or mozzarella cheese
1 teaspoon oregano
garlic salt
4 teaspoons grated Parmesan cheese

Cut rolls in half. Pour pizza sauce over bottom half of rolls. Arrange three meatballs, sliced in half, on each, then sprinkle with oregano and garlic salt. Top with a slice of muenster or mozzarella. Add a tablespoon of Parmesan cheese over each. Top with the other half of the roll. Wrap separately in tin foil and bake in a 400-degree oven for about 15 minutes, until the cheese melts.

VARIATIONS:

Replace meatballs with chunks of sausage, ham or any meat that appeals to you. Instead of meat, tuna, shrimp, lobster or other seafood are good substitutes. Try basil instead of oregano.

Broiled Fish Pizza

MAKES ENOUGH FOR 2–3 SERVINGS

4 one-pound fish fillets (flounder or any other
   boneless fish)
¼ cup melted butter or margarine
1 can pizza sauce
1 cup grated mozzarella cheese
salt and pepper to taste

Brush both sides of fish with butter or margarine.
Season to taste. Broil 5 minutes on each side. Pour
pizza sauce over fish and top with grated mozzarella.
Broil again 7 inches from flame until cheese turns light
brown. Serve.

VARIATIONS:

Use a packaged bread stuffing, prepared as package
instructions direct. Allow ¼ cup stuffing for each fish.

Place fillets over stuffing. Pour pizza sauce over fish, top with grated mozzarella cheese. Sprinkle a little oregano, thyme, basil or tarragon on top. Bake in a 350-degree oven until fish flakes and cheese turns golden brown (about 30 minutes). Serves four.

Sprinkle ¼ cup grated Parmesan on top of fish before baking. Top with drained canned mushrooms, chopped parsley or sliced onion rings before placing fish in oven.

Sauté ¼ cup almonds (thinly sliced, slivered or whole) in oil or butter. Sprinkle the almonds over the fish after removing from oven.

Seafood serves as a savory base for traditional pizza ingredients.

Chicken Pizza Fillets

4 large chicken fillets (chicken breasts, boned and
  skinned)
1 can pizza sauce
1 cup sliced mushrooms
1 eight-oz. package mozzarella cheese, shredded
2 teaspoons oregano
4 teaspoons Parmesan cheese, grated
salt and pepper to taste

To the fancier of mushrooms, cheese, herbs and
chicken, this main-dish pizza is a unique adventure
in taste.

Place fillets in a 10-inch pie pan. Pour pizza sauce
over top. Scatter mushrooms over all. Sprinkle mozzarella cheese on top of mushrooms. Season with
oregano, salt and pepper, and top with Parmesan
cheese. Bake in moderate oven, 350 degrees, uncovered, for about 35 minutes.

VARIATIONS:

Prepare packaged stuffing according to directions. Place fillets over 3 tablespoons of stuffing each, or more if you prefer. Replace oregano with sage, basil or thyme in above recipe. Bake in 350-degree oven for about 35 minutes.

Before placing prepared chicken in oven, sprinkle top with sliced onion rings. Bake as directed.

Sprinkle ¼ cup sautéed, slivered nuts over chicken after removing from oven.

Use above recipe with veal instead of chicken, and add desired variations.

Mel's Pizza Omelette

2 tablespoons butter or olive oil

3 eggs, beaten

5 tablespoons tomato sauce

4 strips (about 2 by 3 inches) mozzarella or Muenster cheese

5 anchovy strips (optional)

1 teaspoon oregano

1 tablespoon Parmesan cheese

In a 6-inch skillet, heat olive oil, or melt butter until bubbly. Pour beaten eggs into hot fat. As eggs begin to set, spoon tomato sauce onto eggs in polka dot fashion by the tablespoon, without mixing. Place cheese on top of eggs and sauce, with one slice in the center. Lay one anchovy slice on each of the cheese slices. For design effect, place the center anchovy down in an O-form. Sprinkle with oregano and Parmesan cheese. Cover skillet and cook on medium-low heat until eggs are set and cheese melts.

Pizza Burger

MAKES ONE SERVING

¼ pound ground chuck or your favorite ground
  meat
garlic and onion salt
1 tablespoon tomato sauce for each hamburger
1 slice Muenster cheese for each hamburger
oregano
1 onion slice or 1 teaspoon fried onion for each
  hamburger
Parmesan cheese

Shape meat patties. Broil meat on both sides, leaving
the center slightly raw. Season with garlic and onion
salt. Spoon sauce over each; top with cheese, oregano,
onion and Parmesan cheese. Bake in 375-degree oven
until cheese melts, or broil until cheese bubbles.

Salami Pizza Sandwich

MAKES 8–10 SERVINGS

1 cup pizza sauce
1 loaf Italian bread,
   cut in half
   lengthwise
12 slices salami
8 slices Muenster
   cheese
½ cup Bermuda
   onion, sliced into
   rings

½ cup sliced ripe,
   pitted olives
½ cup grated
   Parmesan cheese
oregano
salt and pepper to
   taste

Spread pizza sauce on bottom half of bread. Top with salami, Muenster cheese, onion, olives, Parmesan cheese and seasoning. Cover with other half of bread. Bake in 450-degree oven for 5 minutes, or until hot.

VARIATIONS:

Replace salami with one or a combination of any of the following: meatballs (canned or homemade); sliced tongue or other coldcuts; cooked chicken or turkey slices; rare roast beef; thin slices fried steak; quick-fried veal; tuna, shrimp, anchovy fillets, sardines, salmon or other fish; cooked frankfurters or sausages; fried peppers; sliced hard-cooked eggs; fried eggplant slices.

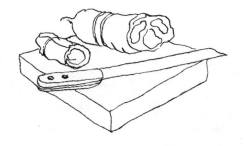

Pizza Parisienne

MAKES ONE 9-INCH PIE

1 partially baked
  9-inch pastry shell
4 medium sliced
  tomatoes or
  equivalent canned,
  drained, sliced
  tomatoes
2 tablespoons onion
  flakes
1½ cups ricotta or
  cream style cottage
  cheese
1 cup shredded
  mozzarella cheese

3 eggs
½ cup cooked ham,
  cut into small
  pieces
2 tablespoons
  chopped parsley
salt and pepper to
  taste
¼ cup grated
  Parmesan cheese
1 can anchovy fillets

Arrange tomatoes evenly in bottom of pie shell in pan. Mix remaining ingredients together, except

Parmesan cheese and anchovies. Pour mixture into pastry shell. Place anchovy fillets over pie in pinwheel fashion. Sprinkle with Parmesan cheese. Bake in 375-degree oven for 40 minutes or until top is puffed and browned. To test, insert knife blade. It should come out clean.

VARIATIONS:

Add other meats such as cooked, drained Italian sausage; sliced pepperoni; chopped meat; prosciutto; salami or frankfurter slices.

Eliminate all meat and substitute this: shrimp, chopped clams, lobster or other fish of your choice.

Omit all meat and fish and substitute ½ cup coarsely chopped nuts. After about 20 minutes of baking, or when the pie sets on top, pour a small can of tomato sauce over surface for a special pizza taste.

This recipe is a variation of the famous French dish, quiche.

Pizza Fondue

1 garlic clove
1 tablespoon
  cornstarch
1½ tablespoons
  oregano
salt and pepper to
  taste
½ cup dry white wine
¼ cup kirsch
2 cups tomato sauce

2 cups mozzarella
  cheese, shredded
½ cup sharp Cheddar
  cheese
½ cup Parmesan
  cheese
French or Italian
  bread, cut into
  1-inch cubes

Rub the inside of a chafing dish with the peeled and halved garlic clove. Mix cornstarch with oregano, seasoning and liquids. Pour mixture into chafing dish. Heat until bubbles appear on surface. Do not boil. Blend in cheeses and stir until smooth and melted.

To serve, offer each guest a long-handled fork to spear into a piece of bite-sized French or Italian bread.

The bread is then dunked into the fondue, coating all sides and eaten when cool enough.

VARIATIONS:

Blend in 2 tablespoons anchovy paste with the liquids.

Use bread sticks for dipping into fondue. Bite off the dunked end, dip again and continue this way until the bread stick is eaten.

Try bite-sized pieces of toast for dunking instead of other bread.

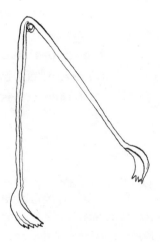

Potato Pizza

MAKES ENOUGH FOR A DEEP 10-INCH PIE

3 medium potatoes,
 cooked and mashed
1¼ cups flour
salt and pepper to
 taste
4 tablespoons olive oil
1 cup drained, canned
 plum tomatoes
2 fresh basil leaves or
 ½ teaspoon dried
 leaves

½ cup mozzarella
 cheese shredded or
 diced
2 tablespoons
 Parmesan cheese,
 grated
1 teaspoon oregano
6 anchovies (optional)

Mix flour and salt into potatoes. Combine thoroughly. Spread into bottom of greased pan. Use half the oil over the top of the potato mixture. Add a layer of tomatoes, the basil, top with mozzarella and Parmesan cheese. Scatter oregano over surface, sprinkle the remaining oil over all. Arrange anchovies as a last touch (optional). Bake in hot oven 400 degrees F. for about ½ hour or until the cheese melts and turns light brown. Serve hot. Enough for 4 to 6 servings.

VARIATIONS:

Sprinkle 2 tablespoons fresh chopped parsley over pie surface while still hot from the oven.

Sprinkle 2 tablespoons capers over pie either before or after baking.

Spinach Pizza

MAKES ONE 13-INCH PIE

1 medium onion,
 sliced
½ cup sliced
 mushrooms
3 tablespoons oil
1 cup chopped frozen
 spinach
salt and pepper to
 taste

½ cup prepared
 tomato sauce
½ cup sliced or
 shredded
 mozzarella cheese
¼ cup Parmesan
 cheese
1 unbaked pizza pie
 shell

Sauté onion with mushrooms until onion becomes transparent. Add spinach and seasoning, cook 5 minutes more on medium heat. Set aside. Spread tomato sauce over pie shell. Add the mixture of spinach, onions and mushrooms over tomato sauce. Arrange the mozzarella cheese over the top, then sprinkle with Parmesan cheese. Bake on the lower shelf of hot oven (450 degrees F.) for about 15 to 20 minutes when cheese melts and crust turns golden brown. Serve hot. Enough for three servings.

VARIATION:

Instead of mozzarella cheese, crumble ½ cup feta cheese over top of pie.

Pesto Pizza

MAKES ONE 13-INCH PIE

2 cups chopped fresh
  basil leaves
¼ cup olive oil
2 tablespoons   .
  chopped parsley,
  Italian if available
1 tablespoon chopped
  garlic
½ teaspoon salt
freshly ground pepper
  to taste

¼ cup pignoli nuts,
  walnuts as a second
  choice
¼ cup Parmesan or
  pecorino cheese,
  grated
1 tablespoon water
7 pitted black olives,
  sliced
1 freshly baked
  13-inch pie crust

Blend the first nine ingredients in the container of an electric blender. When smooth remove from blender and spread over baked pie crust. Sprinkle top with black olives. Slice and serve while crust is still warm. Makes about two to three servings.

VARIATIONS:

Top pie with six strips of anchovies.

Top pie with two fresh coarsely chopped medium size tomatoes.

6

INTERNATIONAL PIZZA

$\mathbb{T}$ HIS chapter is a compilation of recipes developed by incorporating familiar ingredients from the national cuisines of many lands and marrying them to pizza dough. Pizza is a citizen of the world. By adding some of the characteristic flavors of other countries to the basic dough we exercise our imagination and ingenuity to create colorful and novel dishes.

Austrian Pizza Schnitzel

MAKES ENOUGH FOR 4 SERVINGS

4 four-ounce slices top quality veal, pounded thin
1 cup flour
½ teaspoon salt
2 eggs, beaten
1 cup fine dry bread crumbs, preferably with
  Italian seasoning
¾ cup shortening, part olive oil
2 medium-sized plastic or paper bags

Out of the frying pan into the plate. Put the flour and salt into one bag, the dry bread crumbs into the other. Coat each cutlet separately. Place meat in bag with flour. Close bag and shake well until meat is coated. Shake off excess. Dip meat into the beaten eggs, covering both sides; then place in the bag with bread crumbs and shake. Fry veal in hot oil until golden brown on each side for a few minutes. Drain on paper towels.

VARIATION:

Top your Pizza Schnitzel as follows:

1 cup marinara sauce (page 50)
½ cup shredded mozzarella cheese
¼ cup Parmesan cheese
oregano

Place cutlets in baking pan. Pour sauce over meat. Top with mozzarella cheese, Parmesan cheese, then sprinkle each with oregano. Bake in 350-degree oven until cheese melts—about 5 minutes. Remove from oven.

Armenian Pizza,
Lahmejoun *or* Missahatz

MAKES 8 SMALL PIES

1 prepared recipe
   Basic Dough I
1 pound ground lamb
   or beef
½ cup chopped green
   pepper
¾ cup chopped
   parsley
1 chopped garlic clove
½ cup chopped onion

1 teaspoon paprika
   with a bit of cayenne
½ teaspoon allspice
salt and pepper to
   taste
1½ cups chopped
   plum tomatoes
2 tablespoons tomato
   paste

Divide dough into eight equal portions. Form into balls, set on lightly-floured board, and cover with plastic wrap or damp tea towel. Wait 15 minutes, then roll each ball out to an 8-inch circle. Place on greased baking sheets. Combine meat, tomatoes, and seasonings; spread equal portions of mixture over surface of each circle. Bake on bottom shelf of oven, preheated to 500 degrees, from 6 to 9 minutes until bottom of dough changes color. Remove baking sheet to top shelf and continue to cook about 5 minutes. Do not overcook. Serve hot or cold.

Armenian pizza is smaller than Italian pizza—about 8 inches in diameter. Fresh, chopped vegetables and seasonings are combined to create this delicious dish.

Chinese Beef with Green Pepper Pizza (Niu Ju Chin Jow)

MAKES ENOUGH FOR 3–4 SERVINGS

1 prebaked pizza shell
½ pound lean steak, sliced thin
4 tablespoons peanut oil
4 green peppers cut into strips
2 scallions cut into 1-inch pieces
1 slice fresh ginger root, cut into thin strips

1 clove garlic, minced
3 tablespoons soy sauce
2 tablespoons dry sherry
½ cup consommé
1 tablespoon cornstarch

Heat 2 tablespoons oil in skillet and quickly fry beef until pink color disappears. Set beef aside; add remaining oil to skillet and fry peppers, scallions, garlic and ginger for 2 minutes. Return beef to pan. Mix soy sauce, sherry, consommé, and cornstarch together and pour into skillet with other ingredients. Cook and stir until sauce becomes thick and transparent. Spoon into prebaked pie shell and place in 350-degree oven for a few minutes to heat the crust through.

French Pizza, Pissaladière

MAKES ENOUGH FOR 3–4 SERVINGS

2 pounds Bermuda onions, sliced
1 clove garlic, chopped
½ cup olive oil
sprinkling of oregano
½ cup grated Parmesan cheese
1 Standard Pastry Dough recipe, partially baked
16 pitted Mediterranean olives
8 anchovy fillets

Sauté onions and garlic in olive oil over low heat until onions are soft, but not browned. Add oregano. Sprinkle Parmesan cheese over partially cooked pastry dough; spread onion mixture on top. Cut remaining pastry into strips and make lattice design on top of onions. Place an olive in center of each square. Decorate with anchovies. Bake in preheated 400-degree oven on middle shelf for about 15 minutes, or until crust turns golden brown and center begins to bubble.

Greek Pizza, Tiropitta

MAKES ONE 12-INCH PIE

2 eggs
1 cup feta cheese, crumbled
1 cup cottage cheese, small curd or 1 cup ricotta
2 tablespoons butter, melted
1 tablespoon milk
1 unbaked 12-inch pizza pie shell

Beat eggs until thick. In another bowl, mix cheeses with butter and milk. Beat into eggs. Spread mixture onto pie shell, Bake in preheated 400-degree oven on lowest shelf until shell is golden brown—about 25 minutes.

A Greek variation using pizza dough instead of phyllo sheets.

Greek

Taramosalata *Pizza*

MAKES ENOUGH FOR 6 SERVINGS

1 four-ounce jar tarama (salted carp roe)
1 medium onion
juice of 2 lemons
5 slices white bread, crusts removed
1 cup olive oil
1 pizza pie shell, freshly baked

In blender, combine tarama, onion and lemon juice. Blend until smooth. Moisten bread in hot water and squeeze dry. Tear moistened bread into pieces. Add to blended mixture and blend well again. Slowly pour the oil in while blending until no trace of oil is left. Spoon into baked pie shell; spread to edge of pie. Decorate with a bit of parsley in the center and serve.

East Indian Curried Pizza

MAKES ENOUGH FOR 3–4 SERVINGS

1 cup onions, chopped
2 tablespoons shortening
1½ cups meat, fish or poultry, cooked and cut into small pieces
¼ cup crystalized ginger, slivers
½ cup mushrooms, fresh or canned
2 tablespoons curry powder
¼ teaspoon powdered cloves

1 teaspoon minced garlic
salt and pepper to taste
2½ tablespoons all-purpose flour
1¼ cups meat stock
1 tablespoon lemon or lime juice
½ cup light sweet cream
1 unbaked 13-inch pizza pie shell

Cook onions in shortening in large skillet. When limp and golden, mix in meat, ginger, mushrooms, spices and flour. Blend in liquids, stirring constantly. Cook until thickened. Pour into unbaked pie shell. Bake in 450-degree oven on lowest shelf until crust turns golden brown, about 15 to 20 minutes. Serve with a choice of condiments to be scattered on top of the pizza: banana slices, chopped peanuts, raisins, crisp bacon bits, flaked coconut, chutney, pineapple bits, chopped onion, or chopped egg.

Pizza Tel Aviv

MAKES ENOUGH FOR 4 SERVINGS

4 round matzos
2 teaspoons grated onion
½ teaspoon salt
3 eggs, beaten

Place matzos under cool running water. When softened, drain and place in a round shallow dish. Add salt and onion to beaten egg and pour over matzos. Soak for 10 minutes. Fry matzos on both sides until lightly browned. Don't overcook.

PIZZA TEL AVIV TOPPING

1 cup tomato sauce
1 cup cottage cheese

**1 schmaltz herring, boned and cut into
   small pieces**

Spread ¼ cup tomato sauce on each matzo. Sprinkle
cottage cheese over surface. Scatter herring bits over
top. Bake in 350-degree oven for 8 minutes.

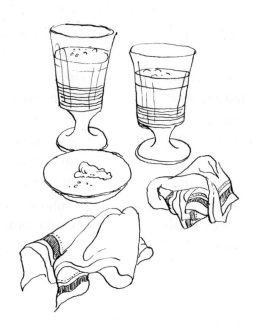

Mexican Pizza Sombrero

MAKES 4–6 SLICES

¾ pound chopped
   meat
1 cup tomato sauce
1 peeled chopped
   tomato
1 teaspoon chili
   powder
½ teaspoon cumin
   powder
½ teaspoon garlic
   powder
½ teaspoon salt

1 teaspoon sugar
1 tablespoon lemon
   juice
1 15½-ounce can
   refried beans
1 cup Cheddar cheese
¼ cup canned
   California chilies,
   chopped
1 avocado, thinly
   sliced

Prepare any Basic Dough recipe from Chapter 1, omitting 3 tablespoons flour and replacing with 3 tablespoons yellow corn meal.

Prepare pizza shell for 12-inch pie. Grease pie pan,

sprinkle with additional corn meal. Spread dough over this. Shape pie shell with ½-inch lip at edges.

Brown meat; drain liquid. Mix tomato sauce with spices and lemon juice; add to meat. Simmer, uncovered, 15 minutes. Spread a layer of refried beans over dough, then a layer of meat and sauce. Top with cheese. Scatter chilies over surface. Bake in 450-degree oven, on bottom shelf, 15 to 20 minutes, or until crust turns golden brown. Serve hot with a helping of lettuce, onion, avocado on top.

Polish Pizza

MAKES ONE 12-INCH PIZZA

1 pint sour cream
1 teaspoon horseradish
1 cup sliced mushrooms, sautéed lightly
1 medium onion, minced
1 12-inch unbaked pie shell
1 small can sauerkraut
1 cup sliced kielbasi
caraway seeds

Mix sour cream, horseradish, mushrooms and onion together. Spread over unbaked pie shell. Scatter sauerkraut over surface. Top with sliced kielbasi. Sprinkle with caraway seeds. Bake in 450-degree oven for about 20 minutes, or until dough turns golden brown.

Polynesian Pizza

MAKES ENOUGH FOR 3–4 SERVINGS

1 can hearts of palm,
    cut into bite-size
    pieces
1 cup small pineapple
    chunks
1 cup sea scallops,
    halved or quartered
¼ cup fresh lime juice
2 tablespoons soy
    sauce

1 minced garlic clove
1 twelve-inch pie shell,
    prebaked for 10
    minutes
1 cup dairy sour cream
1 cup shredded
    coconut

Mix the first 6 ingredients together. Marinate for 15 minutes. Strain any leftover juice into sour cream and blend together. Spread sour cream mixture over prebaked pie shell surface. Strew the marinated ingredients over the top. Sprinkle coconut evenly over pie. Bake in 450-degree oven for 10 minutes or until crust turns golden brown.

Scandinavian Smorgasbord Pizza

Bake a 13-inch pie shell using any Basic Dough recipe. Spread a cup of sour cream on the crust. Mark pie into 4 equal triangular sections. The following ingredients are then arranged on separate sections—smorgasbord style.

First Section
4 thin slices smoked salmon
1 medium sliced tomato
4 slices Bermuda onion
1 three-ounce package cream cheese, rolled into half-inch balls
a few small sprigs dill

Second Section
1 cup tiny cooked shrimp
3 thin slices lemon, twisted to form an 8

2 tablespoons chopped parsley or chives

Third Section
about 10 pieces pickled herring
4 slices Bermuda onion, separated
1 sliced hard-cooked egg
5 pimiento strips

Fourth Section
3 slices Swiss cheese
3 slices ham
sliced pickles

On the First Section, spread smoked salmon and tomato slices. Scatter onion slices on top. Place cream cheese balls in strategic places. On the Second Section, arrange tiny shrimp in a row. Slice lemon half way through and twist around. Garnish shrimp with lemon. Sprinkle with chopped parsley or chives. Third Section place pickled herring in this section. Scatter onion on top. Put sliced cooked egg over open areas. Decorate with pimiento strips. On Fourth Section arrange Swiss cheese over sour cream. Fold edges to shape when necessary. Fold ham into triangles. Place over cheese. Garnish with sliced pickle.

Calzone

MAKES SIX TO EIGHT SERVINGS

I consider calzone a pizza relative. The dough is the same as the basic pizza dough. It is folded in half, filled with a choice of various fillings, pinched together to close and baked.

Use Basic Dough I recipe from Chapter 2. Cut dough into 6 or 8 pieces depending on the size you want. Divide the stuffing ingredients into 6 or 8 equal parts. Set aside. Shape each piece of dough into a ball and roll out to desired size. Spread ingredients over pizza. Fold each disk in half and press firmly together to contain stuffing securely. Bake in 450-degree oven as you would a regular pizza, about 20 minutes or until golden. Serve hot.

SUGGESTED CALZONE FILLING: MOZZARELLA CHEESE

½ pound diced mozzarella cheese
¼ pound slivered prosciutto
⅛ pound Italian salami, slivered

salt and pepper to taste
2 cups tomato sauce (optional)
2 tablespoons Parmesan cheese (optional)

May be eaten right from oven or with tomato sauce and Parmesan cheese on top.

Proceed as previously instructed.

RICOTTA CHEESE FILLING:

For each calzone use ⅓ to ½ cup ricotta cheese, a pinch of oregano, salt and pepper to taste. Fold in half and proceed with baking as instructed.

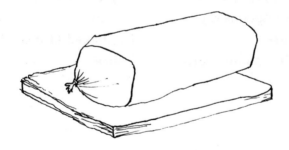

Oriental Pizza

MAKES ONE 13-INCH PIZZA PIE

3 medium onions,
peeled and sliced
2 tablespoons oil
½ cup pineapple,
crushed or small
chunks
1 chopped garlic clove
2 tablespoons soy
sauce
2 tablespoons sherry
wine

¼ teaspoon ginger or
1 teaspoon chopped
fresh ginger
½ cup cooked diced
chicken, shrimp,
ham, or any
preferred fish or
meat
1 unbaked 13-inch pie
shell

Sauté onion in oil in skillet until transparent. Remove from heat. Mix in all other ingredients. Spread over unbaked pizza pie shell. Bake on lower shelf of hot oven at 450-degrees F., until crust turns golden brown, about 15 to 20 minutes. Serve hot. Makes about three servings.

Pizza Flambée

We conclude with the *pièce de résistance* of all variations on a Pizza—a unique and dramatic way to serve pizza for company. Any of the pizza fillings and toppings in the foregoing can be flambéed.

Shortly before serving time, pour ⅓ cup brandy, rum or kirsch into a vessel and heat. Pour the warmed spirit over the pizza, fresh from the oven. Avert your face and ignite. When the flame subsides, cut into serving pieces. Unforgettable.

INDEX